BUSINESS AND
ADMINIST
LEVEL 2

BY TEGAN MARSHALL

BUSINESS AND ADMINISTRATION

LEVEL 2

BUS36 – Principles of providing administrative services

Questions

1.1 – Describe the features of different types of meetings.

1.2 – Outline the different ways of providing administrative support for meetings.

1.3 – Explain the steps involved in organising meetings.

2.1 – Describe the features of different types of business travel and accommodation.

2.2 – Explain the purpose of confirming instructions and requirements for business travel and accommodation.

2.3 – Explain the purpose of keeping records of business travel and accommodation.

3.1 – Describe the features of hard copy and electronic diary systems.

3.2 – Explain the purpose of using diary systems to plan and co-ordinate activities and resources.

3.3 – Describe the types of information needed to manage a diary system.

3.4 – Explain the importance of obtaining correct information when making diary entries.

4.1 – Describe different types of office equipment.

4.2 – Explain the uses of different types of office equipment.

4.3 – Describe factors to be considered when selecting office equipment to complete tasks.

4.4 – Describe how to keep waste to a minimum when using office equipment.

5.1 – Describe the types of mail services used in business organisations.

5.2 – Explain the need for different types of mail services.

5.3 – Explain the factors to be considered when selecting mail services.

5.4 – Explain the factors to be taken into account when choosing postage methods.

6.1 – Describe different types of customers.

6.2 – Describe the impact of their own behaviour on a customer.

6.3 – Explain the impact of poor customer service.

Answers

1.1– Describe the features of different types of meetings? There is a project meeting that brings people from different departments working on specific tasks together. There is a staff meeting which keeps each other informed of what's going on throughout the business. Formal meetings that usually happen when the business or someone inside a business that wants to achieve a good thorough verbal interaction. Then there are informal meetings that are just common meetings usually decided within minutes that it's going to happen rather than being planned and organised. Lastly, there is an AGM. This is for the general membership of an organisation conference that can usually take part for days.

1.2– Outline different ways of providing administrative support for meetings? Some ways of providing administrative support for meetings are finding out basic details of meetings, what type of meeting it is, how much money is going to be spent on this meeting, the number of people going to the meeting, where the meeting is held etc. Also, finding out the aim of the meeting and why there having it, find out the roles of the people who are attending the meeting and lastly organise a checklist so that other meetings don't conflict with each other.

1.3– Explain the steps involved in organising meetings? Firstly, set the proper date, time and venue and inform everybody about it then prepare the agenda, summarise the previous meetings and what has changed in the time from the last one till this one. Prepare all meeting rooms with computers, chairs, tables and stationary etc. Also it would be good to make yourself available to take notes in the meeting.

2.1 – Describe the features of different types of business travel and accommodation? The main types of business travel are car (company car), taxi, train, coach, boat or airplane. Accommodation for business can vary between a cheap bed and breakfast or a luxury hotel. Some businesses have their own accommodations.

2.2 – Explain the purpose of confirming instructions and requirements for business travel and accommodation? You can confirm the travel by checking the times you're leaving, the times you're coming back and the pick up and drop off location etc. You can confirm accommodation by checking the location of the accommodation, the payment arrangements and the type of the accommodation you're staying at. The purpose is to know where you're travelling from, have the correct times for everything, and know where you're traveling to and to take the correct documentation.

2.3 – Explain the purpose of keeping records of business travel and accommodation? Keeping destination dates and costs all is good because it is important for taxation of the company, for insurance purposes and lastly to record as part of the company's account.

3.1 – Describe the features of hard copy and electronic diary systems? Hard copy diaries are hand written, they are portable but not easy to change if some information has changed. If you make a mistake and you only have one copy then you're going to have to write it all out again or it would look really messy. Hard copy diaries are a bad idea. Electronic diary system are much better because they really easy to change, you get automatic notifications of reminders, everything is always saved and backed up so you won't ever loose it. It can't get damaged and if it does you've got a back up copy, you can also send things to several people at once which saves a lot of time.

3.2 – Explain the purpose of using diary systems to plan and co-ordinate activities and resources? To plan it is mainly time management. Without that administration staff would have to spend an exhausting amount of time trying to co-ordinate people diary's in order to schedule meetings, deliveries etc. A diary system on a network allows meetings to be scheduled when the majority of people are available, can remind people to attend the meetings, can schedule deliveries at appropriate time for a process to run efficiently. They can also document the plan of the meeting, so you know who can be expected to be where and when, and what they have been asked to bring with them.

3.3 – Describe the types of information needed to manage a diary system? You need dates, times, venues, who the people are involved, how your travelling so you can keep some time available before and after the event. These are all needed to manage a diary system.

3.4 – Explain the importance of obtaining correct information when making diary entries? All relevant information has to be obtained because you have to make sure that everyone attending the meeting or anyone important has convenience and are given all the details, so that there is no error at any end at any time.

4.1 – Describe different types of office equipment? Firstly, there is office stationary such as pens, notepads, glue stick, books and staplers; these are used in large amounts in various offices. For example sticky notes are used to note down things that are urgent. Computers have become a main part of equipment in any office. They play an important role in many different types of office based work. For example they allow access to the internet. They use of laptops allows people to work from home. Hardware which includes printers and scanners is useful in many daily office operations also.

4.2 – Explain the use of different types of office equipment? The computer allows you to access to the internet which enhances emails, chats and skype. It allows you to prepare documents and prepare and save accounts information. The printer is used to print hard copies of the documents saved onto the computer. The stationary is used to write down important things, urgent things, dates, times and meetings etc.

4.3 – Describe factors to be considered when selecting office equipment to complete tasks? Consider safety, such as desks. Desks should be safe to work from, glass topped and sharp edges are very unsafe. Consider the appropriateness of a task, for example, using a computer at work instead of a laptop but taking a laptop home to work from there. Lastly consider the costs; everything should be within the budget of the company.

4.4 – Describe how to keep waste to a minimum when using office equipment? Don't print more than you need to and make sure you're printing the correct thing so you don't have to reprint it, this saves paper. Photo copying back to back also saves a lot of paper also. If there is any paper not needed, recycle. Use mechanical pencils so only the lead needs to be replaced, not the whole pencil.

5.1 – Describe the types of mail services used in business organisations? Firstly, there is external mail, which is between people who are typically not in the same location. External mail is often addressed to a particular person and may not be an exchange of information. Often used to keep the lines of communication open for business proposes. External mail is not as quick and typically reply's on the postal service. Can be in the form of an email and this is sometimes as quick as internal mail. Internal mail is less formal than correspondence that is sent outside the business. Maybe between people who are in close proximity or opposite ends of the building, used to share information between one or more recipients. Exchange is very quick when email is used.

5.2 – Explain the need for different types of mail services? Because some mail needs to be sent quicker than others, if it's quite far away it's easier to send an email rather than a letter. This way is cheaper than printing off loads of paper and then posting it all. It is cheaper to send out a letter in the post than use a courier company as you can post a letter but petrol money may cost a lot more.

5.3 – Explain the factors to be considered when selecting mail services? When selecting mail services you should consider cost of posting a letter or the cost of using a courier company. Consider the speed, which ones going to be faster to send and deliver. Consider security, which ones more confidential and safer.

5.4 – Explain the factors to be taken into account when choosing postage methods? The cost needs to be considered, the size of the item being posted, the value of the item, how quickly the delivery can be made, if it is a secure method or if they need it signed for.

6.1 – Describe the different types of customers? Internal customers are people that work within your organisation, maybe directly with you or in another department, these could be managers, cleaners, colleagues, drivers etc. External customers are people you normally consider as customers. They come from outside the business you work for. They bring in the revenue that keeps companies afloat.

6.2 – Describe the impact of their own behaviour on a customer? The way you look and behave impacts directly on how satisfied the customer is. You need to be confident, friendly, and caring. Good approach towards customers is crucial. If you do not bring this, the customer may not return. Be welcoming, polite and helpful so the customer feels valued and give a positive impression of the organisation. If you have negative impact then customers will look elsewhere for business. Show interest because if not the customer may not feel valued.

6.3 – Explain the impact of poor customer service? Current customers may not want to come to you anymore, you may loose any potential customers that want to work with you, you may loose future customers because the might be told what the people within your business are like. You will loose your reputation which that alone will stop or decrease your customers, loss of employees because they may feel they don't want to work for you anymore and then finally all this then equals to a loss of profit for your business as you have less customers and less employees trying to get more customers.

BUS37 – Principles of business document production and information management

Questions

1.1 – Describe different types of business documents that may be produced and the format to be followed for each.

1.2 – Explain the use of different types of information communication technology (ICT) for document production.

1.3 – Explain the reasons for agreeing the use, content, layout, quality standards and deadlines for document production.

1.4 – Explain the importance of document version control and authorisation.

1.5 – Explain how the requirements of security, data protection, copyright and intellectual property legislation may affect the production of business documents.

1.6 – Explain how to check the accuracy of business documents.

2.1 – Explain how the requirements of security, data protection, copyright and intellectual property legislation may affect the distribution and storage of business documents

2.2 – Describe different types of distribution channels.

3.1 – Describe the types of information found in business organisations.

3.2 – Explain the need for safe storage and efficient retrieval of information.

3.3 – Describe the features of different types of systems used for storage and retrieval of information.

3.4 – Describe the legal requirements for storing business information.

Answers

1.1– Describe different types of business documents that may be produced and the format to be followed for each? Firstly there is a report, any document that is written to explain a project, provide facts or general information. Then there is letters, a formal letter is a type of correspondence from an organisation to a client or other contact. There is email which is used for business purposes a business email should always end with a signature. Then there is minutes, minutes of a meeting or a summary of what was discussed and the decisions made, it should follow the same structure of agenda. Lastly there is memo's which are short notes to someone else in the same organisation.

1.2– Explain the use of different types of information communication technology for document production? Firstly there is a template which is a simple document that can be completed by hand or through a software assistant. These include company response letters. Then there is spread sheets which is for storing, calculating, filtering, verifying, sorting, displaying, creating graphs etc. Lastly there are slide shows that are on screen presentations of information of ideas presented on slides, Also you can get customized software which deals with the payroll.

1.3– Explain the reasons for agreeing the use, content, layout, quality standards and deadlines for document production? If the purpose is unclear the writing will not make as much sense as it needs too, loopholes may arise as clients requirements are not documented properly. This may invalidate the terms of agreement if it is distributed, content is fairly same. When objects and deadlines are set it is easier to do the research. Research should know what kind of information is needed, how detailed it would be, what form it should be presented in and when the research has to be ready. If objectives and deadlines are not set, researcher could be blamed and probably the research will have to be done all over again.

1.4– Explain the importance of document version control and authorisation? Version control helps to preserve the authenticity of a document or record. One version can easily be distinguished from any subsequent copies. Policy, procedure and guidelines within NHS file go through various literation's before being endorsed and approved for distribution, and once published will often be amended and re-released a number of times. By ensuring that version control is used on all documents, it will assist in providing an audit trail for future tracking of document development.

1.5– Explain how the requirements of security, data protection, and copyright and intellectual property legislation may affect the production of business documents? Firstly we have security. Information does not breach security protocols, if security breach production may need to be minimised or stopped. Storing of business documents may need to be moved. Secondly data protection. Information is fairly and accurately processed, documents may need to be authorised by a manager, produced and communicated on a secure system. Then there is copyright. Permission to use copyrighted material. Need to be authorised by managers or other departments may need to be sought. Lastly there is intellectual property. Agreements covering ownership of partners. Authorisation by manager or other departments may also need to be sought. The affect of all this is it will take longer, other people or departments may need to be involved, agreements needed from multiple parties.

1.6– Explain how to check the accuracy of business documents? Firstly check your facts, double check any statistics, numbers, dates, names, spellings and other facts within a reliable source. Secondly use spell check, running spell check when your done writing is an important step to ensure accuracy. Next use a style guide; these are often overlooked details that give your documents a professional edge. Lastly find an objective reader, asking someone else to read your text is the best way of ensuring your intended meaning is clearly communicated to your readers.

2.1 – Explain how the requirements of security, data protection, copyright and intellectual property legislation may affect the distribution and storage of business documents? Firstly security may affect storing business documents because there are physical conditions and locations for paper documents. There is network or remote archive storage for electronic documents. You can back up arrangements for electronic documents. You can archive policy for identifying storage documents and there is a restricted status. Secondly security may affect distribution because there is the use of secure electronic sites. They use secure systems with public distributions such as the post office and also the use of private couriers. Then there is data protection which may affect the storage of business documents which has restricted access, has the length of time information may be kept for. Data protection may affect distribution such as confidential information to authorised recipients only, international restrictions for sending information covered by data protection requirements. Copyright may affect distribution because of the length of time information may be kept for. Copyright may affect the storage of business documents because materials are clearly identified. Intellectual property may affect the storage because of the length of time information may be kept for and finally intellectual property may affect distribution because materials are clearly identified as being the intellectual property of an organisation or individual.

2.2 – Describe different types of distribution channels? Documents sent through email or intranet services are called electronic distribution channels, these show names of recipients and the sender is seen. Can send to multiple recipients and can send through attachments, and are password protected. Documents sent through internal distribution or external distribution is called paper distribution channels. These are convenient, documents for sign off can be sent, also there is no cost for internal distribution.

3.1 – Describe the types of information found in business organisations? Transaction processing provides up to date information on different types of transactions. Customer management; customer relationship management systems provide information on customer's preferences and purchasing patterns. Decision support provides managers with access to financial, marketing and operational data that helps them to make better, faster decisions. Supply chain management enables companies to share information via secure networks with suppliers and business partners, improving efficiency and controlling costs through a supply chain service support, where companies can bring together service information in a central database that enables field service teams to access the information they need to complete their work efficiency.

3.2 – Explain the need for safe storage and efficient retrieval of information? The need for safe storage is confidentiality of information, also the regulatory requirements for retraining records. Efficient retrieval is for time saving and speedy retrieval in emergencies. They are well organised and it is because of archiving.

3.3 – Describe the features of different types of systems used for storage and retrieval of information? The types of storage for physical documentation are electronic and paper. Electronic storage is a remote storage of electronic documents; they archive electronic documents on company network and mobile storage for electronic documents. Paper storage is also a remote storage of electronic documents. They archive paper documents off site and on site. The systems they use for retrieval are search procedures. They are password protected for restricted access, they have file naming protocols and access to keys and cards. The process of retrieval is signing documents to go in and out.

3.4 – Describe the legal requirements for storing business information? The data protection requirements say you can only keep the documents for the time they are permitted to be there, the documents are only aloud access by authorised people only and also you have to regularly update the documents to keep them accurate. The financial requirements for storing business information is that the documents are only accessible by authorised people only, and also they are only kept for the recommended amount of time which is usually 7 years for accounts and 50 years for personal records.

BUS34 – Communication in a business environment

Questions

1.1 – Explain why different communication methods are used in the business environment.

1.2 – Describe the communication requirements of different audiences.

1.3 – Explain the importance of using correct grammar, sentence structure, punctuation, spelling and conventions in business communications.

1.4 – Explain the importance of using appropriate body language and tone of voice when communicating verbally.

Answers

1.1 – Explain why different communication methods are used in the business environment? Formal communication can be used for example a written memorandum from a manager to their department. Informal communication is usually delivered by talking to each other face to face. Written communication involves writing letters to people and emails. There is verbal and non verbal communication which means either talking using your voice as in face to face or talking across an email or a letter. Also, body language is a form of communication. For example, if your sat slumped on your chair people are going to assume that your not confident or your not very organised etc but If you are sat upright and looking confident people will want to speak to you more and get help from you as you look confident enough to deal with them. There is c visual communication which includes things like power point presentations, public notices and advertisements. Internal communication is distributed to employees within an organisation and external communication is distributed to an organisations external customers.

1.2 – Describe the communication requirements of different audiences? Internal audiences would be acceptable to communication via face to face or phone and also it would be acceptable to take quite informally as working for the same organisation you will more than likely know person. External audiences such as customers, suppliers or regulatory authorities, it wouldn't be acceptable to talk informally to them it would have to be formal and using business lingo s you have sort of a professional look about you. You could talk to them via phone, email, but the customer's usual expectation is for you to talk with a level of detail and intelligence.

1.3   – Explain the importance of using correct grammar, sentence structure, punctuation, spelling and conventions in business communications? The correct use of grammar in business communication gives a good impression of the writer and the company. A well written letter or email tells the reader that the writer is a person who can be relied upon to do a good job. The reader of such letter can believe that the writer can not only use native language properly, but can conduct business in a good and proper manner. A sloppy letter indicates a sloppy attitude to work, and that is not the way to get and keep customers.

1.4   – Explain the importance of using appropriate body language and tone of voice when communicating verbally? You use tone of voice for making and receiving phone calls, contributing to discussions etc. It is important to use appropriate tone of voice as it is presenting a good image for your self and the company; it also has an impact on others as an example if you have a harsh and stubborn tone of voice you may loose customers for it. Body language is a language without words, it is a non-verbal communication. It is important to use the correct body language in business because if we didn't were not giving a professional image to yourself, also if you are constantly slouching or moving your hands you do not appear to be confident so it is important to have good body language so customers feel you're confident enough to do the job correctly.

BUS14 – Produce business documents

Questions

1.1 – Explain the requirements for language, tone, image and presentation for different documents.

1.2 – Explain how to integrate images into documents.

1.3 – Describe how corporate identity impacts upon document production.

1.4 – Explain the requirements of data protection, copyright and intellectual property legislation relating to document production.

1.5 – Describe organisational procedures for version control.

1.6 – Describe security requirements relating to document production.

Answers

1.1 The requirements for language are that documents need to be aimed at the correct audiences, formal for a customer and informal for a colleague you know very well. Also, avoid technical terms that the audience may not understand. The requirements for tone in a business are to be quite formal, using full sentences and avoiding slang words. The requirements for image and presentation in a business are to use accurate spelling, grammas and punctuation and to follow corporate guidelines. Business documents include business letters, reports, emails, minutes, instructions or a news letter.

1.2 – To integrate images to documents you find the right image you want to use, make sure the image is the right sixe and fits the document, if it is a video make sure viewers can view the video easily and clearly.

1.3 – Corporate identity means following corporate guidelines on fonts, styles etc, it portrays a consistent image of the organisation. This impacts upon document production as without documents may take longer to produce and also without it other people or departments may need to be involved.

1.4– Explain the requirements of data protection, copyright and intellectual property legislation relating to document production? The requirements for the data protection act 1998 say that information needs to be fairly and accurately processed, documents may need to be authorised by a manager and also produced and communicated on a secure system. The requirements for the copyright, designs and patents act 1988 say you need permission to use copyrighted material and within a business you may need permission off a manager. The requirements for intellectual property are that you need agreements covering ownership of materials and you may need authorisation off a manager.

1.5– Describe organisational procedures for version control? Version control procedures include numbering each version of a document, using version control tables, using the 'draft' watermark and preventing editing of approved documents.

1.6– Describe security requirements relating to document production? Security requirements relating to document production are the storing of business documents. Business documents should be stored in rooms that are either locked or only have restricted access. You should protect important business documents by using a password or making them read only access so no one can edit or change information. Also, you can use screen filters on the computer screen. Make sure information does not breach security protocols and if it is breached, production may need to be minimised or stopped.

BUS4 – Health and safety in a business environment

Questions

1.1 – State health and safety responsibilities of employers.

1.2 – State a persons own responsibilities for health and safety in the business environment.

1.3 – State the occupational health and safety guidelines to be followed when using a keyboard and visual display unit.

1.4 – Explain the importance of complying with health and safety requirements.

2.1 – Identify possible health and safety hazards in the business environment.

2.2 – Describe ways in which accidents can be avoided in the business environment.

2.3 – Outline why it is important to report hazards and accidents that occur in the business environment.

2.4 – Outline organisational emergency health and safety procedures.

Answers

1.1– State health and safety responsibilities of employers? Health and safety responsibilities of employees can include ensuring health and safety at work, maintaining safe systems at work, observing all general and specific health and safety regulations and training staff how to deal with health and safety risks.

1.2– State a persons own responsibilities for health and safety in the business environment? Following all health and safety training provided, reporting any health and safety concerns, co operate with employer to comply with any legal duty in relation to health and safety.

1.3– State the occupational health and safety guidelines to be followed when using a keyboard and visual display unit? By following occupational health and safety guidelines you must ensure chairs can swivel up and down with adjustable back rests, desks must be big enough hold all the equipment, computer screens must be adjustable and not flickering and have regular breaks if you're using a computer for a long time.

1.4– Explain the importance of complying with health and safety requirements? Health and safety requirements include reporting injuries, use of wok equipment, use of personal protective equipment and following health and safety requirements. This is important to follow to ensure all staff safety and to avoid damage of equipment.

2.1 – Identify possible health and safety hazards in the business environment? A hazard is something that may cause harm or damage. Possible health and safety hazards would be unsafe machinery, tangled and visible wires, slippy floors, poor lighting and electrical faults.

2.2 – Describe ways in which accidents can be avoided in the business environment? You can avoid accidents in the work place by following procedures, PAT tests, cleaning spillages, not having liquids near computers, turning off machinery after use and not cluttering desks.

2.3 – Outline why it is important to report hazards and accidents that occur in the business environment? It is important to report hazards in the work place so they get fixed quickly, legal requirements, so everyone is aware it is a hazard and to reduce the risk of future harm.

2.4 – Outline organisational emergency health and safety procedures? People in the office are first aiders if it is needed they can perform first aid, one person in the office is a fire marshal so they perform the procedure if there ever was a fire in the building by ringing the fire bell, evacuating the building and making sure everyone is out of the building and waiting for the fire engine. If anyone needed medical assistance one person in the office would ring a doctor or an ambulance for that individual.

BUS6 – Use a telephone and voicemail system

Questions

1.1 – Outline how caller's experiences affect their view of an organisation.

1.2 – Outline organisational standards and procedures for communicating on the telephone.

1.3 – State the importance of following organisational standards and procedures when making and receiving telephone calls.

1.4 – State organisational fault reporting procedures.

1.5 – Describe why it is important to follow security and data protection procedures when using a telephone system.

1.6   – State the information to be given out when transferring calls, taking or leaving messages.

1.7   – State organisational guidelines for deleting voicemail messages.

Answers

1.1   – Outline how a caller's experiences affect their view of an organisation? Their view is based on what kind of person you're talking too and the impression you make. You have to give the right impression and have good telephone manner, be polite and listen to them. If you meet the caller's needs it will give a good example of the business and generate word of mouth which may result in more revenue for the business. If they get bad experiences in the phone they may consider the whole business to be bad and t may make business loose custom.

1.2   - Outline organisational standards and procedures for communicating on the telephone? Working in administration the organisational standards include using the same greeting in every call, answering after a few seconds, asking what the caller is calling for. Taking their name and writing it down, all this using formal language. Most procedures here include taking messages and transferring calls to different people throughout the workplace and how to take details off the call.

1.3   – State the importance of following organisational standards and procedures when making and receiving telephone calls? It is important to follow standards and procedures so all our staff maintain consistent standards; also it gives a good impression for the business and gives goof customer service. It gives out business a positive reputation and we may make more business.

1.4   - State organisational fault reporting procedures? In my workplace our fault procedure is if we cannot help the customer or answer their questions we should transfer the call to someone who works in the area of business the question relates too. For example, if the question is about stock and I don't know the answer I will transfer it to someone in our sales team. If the phone wasn't working I would have to report it to management who would then ring the phone company and try and get it sorted out, in the meantime if the phone is down we have to take down numbers we need to ring and ring off our personal phones.

1.5   - Describe why it is important to follow security and data protection procedures when using a telephone system? We need to follow security and data protection procedures because of the business sensitive regulations so that the customers or members of staff do not feel offended in any way possible, also we need to maintain a good reputation.

1.6   - State the information to be given out when transferring calls, taking or leaving messages? When transferring calls we need to state the name of the caller and why they are calling and also the purpose of the call. When taking messages we should get the name, date and time, what message it is we are taking and the relevant person whom we are giving the message too. When leaving messages we should state everything we took from the caller and let the person who we are giving the message to know all the information to ensure they understand the message.

1.7   - State organisational guidelines for deleting voicemail messages? At my workplace we have to listen to the voicemail messages every morning, we should then write down all the relevant information e.g. date, time, callers name and what the message actually says. We then pass the message on the relevant person and then we can delete the message. Anyone who opened the voicemail message is authorised to then delete the message after they have got all the information.

CUS13 – Process information about customers

Questions

1.1   – Describe the functions of customer information systems.

1.2   – Explain the way in which legislation and regulatory requirements affect the processing of customer information.

1.3 – Explain different responsibilities and levels of authority for processing customer service information.

1.4 – Explain the reliability of sources of customer information.

1.5 – Explain the validity of customer information.

Answers

1.1– Describe the functions of customer information systems? The types of data organised by an information system include statistics regarding a company's resources, programs, accomplishments and transactions. The most effective information systems process data in real time so managers can make effective decisions with the most up to date information.

1.2– Explain the way in which legislation and regulatory requirements affect the processing of customer information? The data protection act 1998 protects how personal information or data is used and stored. This effects processing customer information because the data is stored according to legislation, sharing of information is restricted and controlled, disclosing of information is confidential.

1.3 – Explain different responsibilities and levels of authority for processing customer service information? Different responsibilities include using things only what they are meant to be used for, keeping information accurate and up to date, not keeping information longer than it is needed to be kept for, keeping data secure and to obtain data fairly. Levels of authority could be staff, managers, supervisors, data controllers or people who have permission.

1.4 – Explain the reliability of sources of customer information? Sources could be customers either internally or externally, suppliers, specialists or records either electronically or on paper. The reliability of resources could either be whether they are trustworthy or qualified, whether they have knowledge or understanding of the sources or if they are relevant.

1.5 – Explain the validity of customer information? The validity means whether it is specifically meets the requirement of the task, if it provides the correct information, if it is up to date or if it is reliable.

BUS26 – Use and maintain office equipment

Questions

1.1 – Describe organisational policies, procedures and levels of authority in maintaining office equipment.

1.2 – Describe how to use different types of office equipment.

1.3 – Explain the reasons for following manufacturers and organisational instructions when operating equipment.

1.4 – Describe the types of equipment faults likely to be experienced and the correct way of dealing with these.

Answers

1.1– Describe organisational policies, procedures and levels of authority in maintaining office equipment? At my workplace when maintaining office equipment we store it all in the filing cupboard, we are able to take anything we need out to use it. We don't have authority to order more supplies and equipment so we just write a list of what we need and email it to management in the head office and they will order it for us.

1.2– Describe how to use different types of office equipment? We use personal equipment such as computers, memory sticks and earphones. We use computers to process business data and send things to people. We use memory sticks by saving data on to them and we use earphones too listen to things that no one else can hear. Shared equipment such as printers and telephones is used by various people. We use printers to print documents off onto paper and we use telephones to keep in contact with people. We also have basic equipment such as paper and pens that we use for everyday things.

1.3– Explain the reasons for following manufacturers and organisational instructions when operating equipment? Reasons for following manufacturers instructions are so you do it correctly and don't break anything and also for troubleshooting. Reasons for following organisational instructions is so you know who can operate the equipment, so you know who you can report a fault too and who can do repairs.

1.4– Describe the types of equipment faults likely to be experienced and the correct way of dealing with these? At my workplace typical faults you have to deal with in the office would be paper jams, paper in the printer running low, toner cartridge running low or connection to the internet lost. By dealing with these faults you follow policies and procedures and let management know about it, they will then decide if we need to ring the tech guys about it or if we can fix it ourselves.

BUS24 – Archive information

Questions

1.1 – describe different ways of archiving information.

1.2 – Describe how to retrieve archived information.

1.3 – Describe organisational procedures for archiving, retrieving and deleting information.

1.4 – Explain the importance of document retention policies to organisations.

1.5 – Describe the security and access requirements of offsite archives.

Answers

1.1– Describe different ways of archiving information? There are lots of different ways to archive information. Firstly you can keep paper copies in files, you can use company systems, for example at my workplace we use OPERA. You can scan things and keep them in a file on the computer or you can have back up files either on the computer or in a filing cupboard etc.

1.2 – Describe how to retrieve archived information? You can retrieve archived information by having access yourself or given permission to access information. By manager authorisation, keeping records or if documents have been taken out of the files or put back. Record when documents where accessed and who by.

1.3 – Describe organisational procedures for archiving, retrieving and deleting information? Archiving – This is organising and storing documents or data but with the ability to retrieve the information if you need to at a different time. Retrieving – This is removing information after it has been archived to a storage system for certain reasons you ma need to see the information during the retention period. Deleting – Permanently destroying documents or data that have been archived previously.

1.4 – Explain the importance of document retention policies to organisations? It limits risks of unauthorised access to information or data, it avoids damage to an organisations business, e.g. competitor, related new product developments, costings. Secure historical information or data and it meets legal requirements.

1.5 – Describe the security and access requirements of offsite archives? You need contract terms with offsite archive organisation which includes confidentiality. You need a secure collection and delivery arrangements. Hard copy archiving, document scanning and file indexing should ass be done correctly and securely. To gain access to information and data you need permission off the allocated accounts manager as they are in charge of archiving documentation or data.

BUS16 – Store and retrieve information

Questions

1.1 – Describe systems and procedures for storing and retrieving information.

1.2 – Outline legal and organisational requirements for information security and retention.

1.3 – Explain how to create filing systems to facilitate information identification and retrieval.

1.4 – Explain how to use different search techniques to locate and retrieve information.

1.5 – Describe what to do when problems arise when storing or retrieving information.

Answers

1.1– Describe systems and procedures for storing and retrieving information? At my workplace we store and retrieve information in 2 different ways. To store information in our filing room we alphabetise it and put it into files in alphabetical order so we can find them easier. We retrieve it by going in and finding it by looking in the files. We also store information in our system on the computer called OPERA; we retrieve it by typing in a password and using the search bar.

1.2– Outline legal and organisational requirements for information security and retention? At my workplace we store business documents in alphabetical ordered files, we have everything backed up and can only access it if your working in the office. We protect data by updating it regularly and we save data on our computer system OPERA. Only people in the office have a password so it is authorised personnel only. Only authorised people are allowed to see our financial requirements such as managers. We keep accounts for 7 years and personal records for 50.

1.3– Explain how to create filing systems to facilitate information identification and retrieval? You can create filing systems in many ways but we save them in alphabetical order. You can also save them chronologically or numerically. You can use document wallets or cabinets or even boxes to file information.

1.4– Explain how to use different search techniques to locate and retrieve information? If using paper bases systems you can use index cards to search techniques to locate and retrieve information or you can use visible edge cards or search alphabetically or numerically. For electronic systems you can use key words or short cuts.

1.5– Describe what to do when problems arise when storing or retrieving information? If you are using manual filing systems you can check the index list to see if it is still on the system, you can check that the information hasn't been filed wrong, also when the file is full, follow company procedures to create a new file. If using electronic filing systems you can check in similar names folders to see if the document has been miss filed, you can carry out a search on the system using keywords or maybe some files may be visible but confidential so only some people can see them.

BUS38 – Understand employer organisations

Questions

1.1 – Explain the differences between the private sector, public sector and voluntary sector.

1.2 Explain the functions of different organisational structures.

1.3 Describe the features of different types of legal structures for organisations.

2.1 – Describe the internal and external influences on organisations

2.2 – Explain the use of different models of analysis in understanding the organisational environment.

2.3 – Explain why change in the business environment is important.

Answers

1.1 – Explain the differences between the private sector, public sector and voluntary sector? Private sectors are run by individuals and companies for profit. They are not state controlled, example: limited companies, sole traders and partnerships. Public sectors are companies which provide various government services, example: schools, police and councils. Voluntary sectors are charities and charitable organisations, example: charities, community groups and housing associations.

1.2– Explain the functions of different organisational structures? There are four main organisational structures which are flat, tall, matrix and functional. For small organisations Flat and functional structures are best as flat structures have only a few people so they are more responsible, and also very flexible. Functional structures are in depth in knowledge of a particular product or area of the company. For large organisations on one site, tall and matric functions are the best as tall structures have more people and are more focused on responsibility. Matrix structures are in depth knowledge of a product within the functional area and have general understanding of other areas of the business. For large organisations across sites or countries, tall and matrix structures are the best as tall structures have more people and more knowledge and matrix structures are in depth knowledge of a product within the functional area and have a better understanding of other areas of the business.

1.3– Describe the features of different types of legal structures for organisation? There are three main legal structures for organisations and they are the public sector, private sector and voluntary sector. Public sectors are set up and controlled by the government and are paid for by taxes that the public pay. Private sectors include sole traders, partnerships and limited companies. Sole traders are one owner who is liable to pay all the debts of the business. Partnerships are shared ownership of a business so they have shared responsibility and joint liability for all debts of business. Limited companies are shared ownership through shareholding investments and the liability is limited to investment in business. Voluntary sectors include unincorporated association, which means they don't have to register with any regulatory body. A charitable trust which is run by a small group of people. A charitable incorporated organisation which is registered and regulated by the charity commission and finally, a charitable company which is a limited company with charitable aims.

2.1 – Describe the internal and external influences on organisations? Internal influences on organisations are communication, manager motivation, company image, reputation, policy making, recruitment processes and management skills. External influences on organisations are lending conditions, interest rates, taxes, government regulations and competition from similar providers.

2.2 – Explain the use of different models of analysis in understanding the organisational environment? SWOT analysis supports planning; it is a very useful framework for analysing your organisations strengths and weaknesses and the opportunities and threats that you face. It helps you focus on your strengths, minimize threats, and take the greatest possible advantage of opportunities available to you. PESTLE analysis examines each factor to assess what the impact or potential impact will be on the organisation. The use of a PESTLE analysis is by marketers to analyse and monitor the macro environmental factors that have an impact on an organisation. The result of this is then used to identify threats and weaknesses which are used in a SWOT analysis.

2.3 – Explain why change in business environment is important?
Change is important in business as it enables a company to meet the dynamic needs of its customers and create growth opportunities. Change also allows a business to keep up with advancing technology and respond to different economic conditions, such as strong or weak economic growth.

Printed in Poland
by Amazon Fulfillment
Poland Sp. z o.o., Wrocław